WRITE THE VISION

THEN

FUND IT

WRITE THE VISION

THEN FUND IT

A KLH Business Solutions Framework for Building Fundable Businesses

Dr. Kara Lock-Harris

KLH Business Solutions
Milwaukee, Wisconsin

This publication is designed to provide accurate and authoritative information in regard to the subject matter covered. It is sold with the understanding that the author and publisher are not engaged in rendering legal, financial, or other professional services. If professional advice is required, the services of a competent professional should be sought. The author and publisher shall not be held liable for any loss or damages resulting from the use of the information contained in this book.

Scripture quotations are taken from the King James Version of the Bible.

Published by KLH Business Solutions LLC

Milwaukee, Wisconsin

www.klhbusinesssolutions.com

ISBN 979-8-9930156-1-3 (Paperback)
ISBN 979-8-9930156-2-0 (eBook / Digital)

First Edition, 2026

Library of Congress Control Number: 2026911726
Printed in the United States of America

Dedication

I dedicate this book first to God, who placed vision inside of me long before I understood what to do with it, and who remained faithful through every transition, every uncertainty, and every moment that required me to trust Him beyond what I could see.

To my mother, whose love, strength, and presence continue to shape me even in her absence. Your life and your words still guide me, and everything I build carries a piece of you within it.

To every entrepreneur who has ever had a vision but did not know where to begin, this book is for you.

And finally, to the version of myself who had to start over — the one who did not plan for the shift but still had to rise. This book is a reminder that what you carry has value, and when it is written, structured, and acted on, it can become something that changes your life and others'.

Write it. Make it plain. Fund it.

Acknowledgments

This book would not exist without the countless entrepreneurs I have had the privilege of walking alongside. Your courage to share your ideas, your willingness to be vulnerable about what you did not know, and your commitment to keep building despite the obstacles — that is what inspired every page of this work.

To my team at KLH Business Solutions — thank you for believing in this mission from the very beginning and for showing up every day with excellence and purpose.

To the mentors, colleagues, and community leaders who poured into me over more than twenty-five years in finance and business — your investment in me became the foundation I stand on.

And above all, to God — who positioned me, prepared me, and made it plain when the time came to build.

Foreword
By Mike A. Williams

Founder & CEO, Brownmine AI | The Executive Translator™

Some books arrive at exactly the right moment. This one was written by someone I have had the privilege of knowing for over ten years, and reading it felt less like reviewing a manuscript and more like finally watching a trusted colleague share what she has been quietly doing for others her entire career.

Dr. Kara Lock-Harris and I met at FIS. I was serving as a Technology Executive. She was a Financial Analyst. From those early conversations, it was obvious that Kara was operating on a different level. She had the discipline of a seasoned finance professional and the instincts of someone who genuinely cared about people getting it right. That combination is uncommon, and it is not something you forget.

Over the years, our careers evolved. The friendship stayed. What has never changed about Kara is her integrity. She is the kind of professional who gives you the honest answer when the comfortable one would have been easier. She is knowledgeable, grounded, and just an overall decent human being in an industry that does not always reward those qualities. When Kara speaks about building a business, people should listen, because she has done the work on both sides of the table.

That is what makes this book worth your time.

Write the Vision, Then Fund It is not about inspiration. It is about execution. Kara takes the vague space between having a great idea and building a fundable business and fills it with structure, clarity, and actionable guidance. She draws from her own experience of navigating a major career transition to build this framework, which means everything in these pages has been pressure-tested in real life.

If you are serious about moving your vision forward, you will not find a more practical, honest, or direct guide than this one. Kara has built something that works, and she has laid it out in a way that meets you wherever you are.

It is my honor to recommend this book and an even greater honor to call its author a friend.

Mike A. Williams
Founder & CEO, Brownmine AI
The Executive Translator™

Table of Contents

Introduction: Write the Vision, Then Fund It 1

PART I — THE AWAKENING.....................................6

Chapter 1: Vision Is Not Enough 7

From Idea to Impact: A Real Example 9

Chapter 2: The Power of Writing It Down 11

What Writing Actually Does for Your Business 12

Writing Reveals What You Do Not Yet Know 12

Chapter 3: The Visibility Problem 14

The Difference Between Being Overlooked and Being Unclear 15

Clarity Is Your Advantage 15

Chapter 4: From Idea to Language...........................17

The Three Foundational Questions 17

What This Looks Like Across Different Businesses ... 18

Refining Your Language Over Time 20

PART II — THE STRATEGY 21

Chapter 5: Make It Plain....................................22

The Reader Test...22

Before and After: What Plain Looks Like 23

Chapter 6: Build the Plan...................................25

Organizational Overview — Who You Are.................25

The Why Behind Your Why — Your Narrative...........26

Statement of Need — The Problem You Solve...........27

Program Design and Activities — How It Works 28

Measurable Outcomes — What Success Looks Like ..29

Budget and Financial Plan — How the Money Is Used 30

Organizational Capacity — Why You Can Do This......31

Sustainability Plan — How It Continues 32

Bringing It All Together 33

Chapter 7: Answering the Money Questions................. 35

How Does Your Business Make Money? 35

Who Is Your Business For? 35

Why Now?... 35

Why You?.. 36

What Happens If This Does Not Work? 36

How Will You Scale? 36

How Funders Actually Think 37

What Makes Funders Say No Quickly 39

Chapter 8: The Clarity Advantage 41

PART III — THE FUNDING BLUEPRINT 44

Chapter 9: The 8 Funding Streams 45

1. Personal Funding.. 45

2. Bootstrapping 46

3. Crowdfunding 47

4. Angel Investors.. 47

5. Grants 48

6. Business Loans 49

7. Partnerships.. 50

8. Venture Capital 51

Chapter 10: Grants — Alignment Over Need 53

Eligibility Is Not the Same as Alignment.................... 53

Where to Find Grant Opportunities 54

Grant Readiness Checklist 55

The Role of a Grant Writer..56

When Funding Is Denied 57

Chapter 11: Building a Fundable Business Foundation . 61

11.1 — Choosing the Right Business Structure 61

11.2 — Registering Your Business Properly................ 62

11.3 — Business Identity Numbers That Matter........ 63

11.4 — Business Credit vs. Personal Credit................. 64

11.5 — Building Strong Business Credit...................... 64

11.6 — Financial Separation and Business Banking... 65

11.7 — Licenses, Permits, and Compliance................. 65

11.7a — Nonprofit Board Governance and Meeting Minutes 65

11.8 — Staying in Good Standing 69

11.9 — Documentation That Funders Expect 70

Funder Readiness Scorecard 70

Chapter 12: Positioning Your Business to Be Seen and Heard.. 73

Your Online Presence... 74

Visibility Is More Than Being Seen 75

Your Elevator Pitch and Beyond................................ 76

The Creative Pitch 77

Chapter 13: Using AI as a Strategic Business Tool 79

What Is Artificial Intelligence? 79

What Is Machine Learning?..80

How AI Learns Your Voice — And How to Help It 80

A Beginner's Guide to Prompting AI 82

AI Tools for Every Stage of Your Business 84

AI for Every Stage of Building Your Business 85

How AI Gives You a Funding Advantage......................87

Identifying Alignment Faster.............................89

PART IV — THE EXECUTION.............................93

Chapter 14: The Vision Worksheet 94

Part 1: Defining Your Vision 94

Part 2: Strengthening Your Position...................95

Part 3: Planning for Growth and Funding..............96

Part 4: Building Sustainability and Structure 97

Chapter 15: Your 30-Day Activation Plan 99

Day 1: Make the Decision 99

Days 2–3: Establish Your Legal Identity................99

Days 4–5: Register and Get Your Numbers 100

Days 6–7: Open Your Business Bank Account..........101

Week 2: Build Your Business Plan.....................101

Week 3: Build Your Visibility.........................101

Week 4: Position for Funding 102

Days 29–30: Review and Recommit 103

Chapter 16: The Discipline of Execution 104

Fear as a Hidden Force 104

Discipline Is the Bridge 105

Chapter 17: From Vision to Legacy.....................107

Legacy Is Built Through Daily Decisions.................107

Impact Is Measured in Service, Not Scale 108

Stewardship 108

Someone Is Waiting for What You Are Building.......109

Continue the Journey.................................111

Services Available Through KLH Business Solutions 111

Glossary of Key Terms 113

Resources Appendix...119

    Business Formation Documents................................119

    Business Registration and Legal Structure 119

    Business Identification Numbers 120

    Licenses and Compliance.. 120

    Grant Funding Opportunities 120

    Business Credit...121

    Small Business Support 121

Common Mistakes to Avoid... 123

    1. Applying for Funding Before the Foundation Is Ready 123

    2. Confusing Eligibility with Alignment 123

    3. Keeping Business and Personal Finances Mixed . 123

    4. Writing the Vision Once and Never Revisiting It. 124

    5. Waiting to Feel Ready Before Taking Action........ 124

    6. Relying Too Heavily on One Funding Source 124

    7. Skipping the Business Plan 124

    8. Letting Inconsistency Become the Pattern............125

About the Author 126

A Note on Sources 128

Introduction: Write the Vision, Then Fund It

"Write the vision, and make it plain upon tables, that he may run that readeth it." — Habakkuk 2:2

There is something powerful about a vision that is written. Not imagined. Not spoken in passing. Not carried quietly in your thoughts. But written, defined, and made plain in a way that others can see, understand, and move with.

For a long time, I did not fully understand the weight of that Scripture in a practical way. I understood it spiritually. I understood it as encouragement. I understood it as something that spoke to purpose. But I had not yet lived it in a way that required me to depend on it. That changed.

For more than twenty-five years, I worked in finance. My career was structured, consistent, and stable. I understood systems. I understood numbers. I understood how businesses operated, how financial statements told a story, and how planning created direction. I built a life around that knowledge. It was familiar, and it was secure.

During that time, I found myself helping others. Friends would come to me with ideas, business concepts, and questions about how to structure what they were trying to build. I would sit with them, listen, and begin organizing their thoughts. I would help them create business plans, map out financial projections, and bring clarity to ideas that felt scattered. It came naturally to me. It was something I enjoyed doing, but I never saw it as something I would need to rely on for myself. I did not realize at the time that I was being prepared.

There is a difference between doing something because you are skilled at it and doing something because you are called to build with it. For years, I operated in the first. But I never considered that one day I would need to take everything I had learned and apply it in a completely different way.

Then everything shifted.

The same industry that had provided stability for years began to change. Technology advanced. Systems became more efficient. Processes that once required people were now being handled by automation. Companies were getting faster, smarter, and more streamlined.

And in that shift, I became one of the people affected.

After decades of experience, after years of building knowledge and working within structured systems, I found myself in a position I had not anticipated. I lost my job due to automation.

What do you do when what you have relied on changes?

What do you do when the system you trusted no longer needs you in the same way?

What do you do when your stability shifts and you are left with a decision?

For a moment, there was uncertainty. Not because I did not have skills, but because I had to see those skills differently. I had to move from using what I knew in a structured environment to building something of my own.

That is where KLH Business Solutions truly came into focus. Automation was not something distant or theoretical. It was happening in real time. In May of 2023, I decided to start KLH Business Solutions as a backup plan. I took the initial steps, established the business, and put the structure in place, but I did not fully build it. I told myself I would come back to it when I had more time. But time has a way of making decisions for you.

By June of 2025, what had once been a backup plan became a necessity. The same shift I had been watching from a distance had reached me personally. I was no longer preparing for change. I was in it. KLH Business Solutions was no longer something I could afford to revisit later. It became something I had to build now.

I had to take my own advice. I had to write my vision. I had to make it plain. I had to structure what I was building in a way that could stand on its own.

And in that process, I saw something clearly. There are many people who have vision, but lack structure. There are many people who have ideas, but do not know how to organize them in a way that others can understand or support. There are many people who want funding, but are not positioned to receive it. It is not because they are not capable. It is because they have not been shown how to move from vision to structure to funding.

That is the gap. And that is why this book exists.

This is not just about starting a business. This is about understanding how to take what you have and build something that is clear, structured, and fundable. Writing the vision is not just a spiritual concept. It is a practical one. When your vision is written, it becomes clear. When it is clear, it can be structured. When it is structured, it can be positioned. And when it is positioned correctly, it can be funded.

You do not need to have everything figured out to begin. You need to be willing to start. You need to be willing to write. You need to be willing to build.

Because what you are carrying is not just an idea. It is a vision. And now it is time to make it plain.

PART I — THE AWAKENING

From Idea to Clarity

Chapter 1: Vision Is Not Enough

"Funding does not respond to excitement. Funding responds to structure."

Your idea is not enough.

I understand that may not feel good to hear, especially if you have been carrying that idea for years. You may have prayed over it, talked about it, and even wrestled with it in private moments. That vision may feel deeply personal, almost sacred. But if we are going to build something that can move beyond conversation and into reality, we have to begin with truth, because truth is what moves you forward.

Every day, I encounter people with powerful ideas. These are not small thoughts or surface-level concepts. I am talking about ideas that have the potential to change families, shift communities, and create real impact. People come to me excited, passionate, full of vision. And I can see it. I can feel it. The potential is there.

But then I ask one simple question. Can you show it to me? Not tell me. Show me.

And in that moment, everything changes. The energy shifts. The confidence softens. What once sounded strong and clear in their mind suddenly becomes difficult to explain out loud. What I see in that moment is not a lack of intelligence or ability. It is a lack of clarity. And clarity is what funding responds to.

Funding does not respond to excitement. Funding responds to structure.

You can have the best idea in the room, but if you cannot explain it in a way that someone else understands quickly and confidently, it will not move. It will remain in conversations, notebooks, and notes saved on your phone. Not because it lacks value, but because it lacks visibility. And what is not visible cannot be funded.

Then the questions begin. What do you do? Who do you serve? How does this make money?

These are not complicated questions, but they require clear answers. If your response becomes uncertain, if you begin circling around your idea instead of defining it, the person on the other side of the table is left without something solid to hold on to. The opportunity begins to close. Not because your idea is not good, but because it cannot be clearly understood.

This is why I say your vision is not enough. Vision is the starting point. It is the spark that initiates movement. But vision alone is not what builds a business. It is not what secures funding, and it is not what creates sustainability. Vision must be translated. It must be written. It must be structured. It must be made plain.

From Idea to Impact: A Real Example

I once worked with a woman I will call Renata. She had been running a natural hair and wellness product line out of her home for three years. She had a loyal customer base, consistent repeat orders, and genuine demand. What she did not have was documentation.

When Renata first came to me, she could not tell me her monthly revenue with confidence. She did not have a written description of her business that she could hand someone. She had never defined her target customer beyond "people who care about natural ingredients." She was talented, hardworking, and passionate — and completely invisible to funders.

We spent several weeks doing what this book teaches you to do. She wrote her vision. She defined her customer precisely. She documented her revenue model. She created a clear one-page business overview. Then we identified a small business grant aligned with women-owned product businesses.

She was awarded $15,000. Not because she suddenly became more talented. She was awarded because she became clear. Her vision, once written and structured, could finally be evaluated. And when it was evaluated, it stood on its own.

So the question is no longer just whether you have a vision. The question becomes whether your vision can speak for you when you are not in the room.

Your idea is not enough. But your idea, when it is written, structured, and made plain, becomes something entirely different. It becomes something that moves. It becomes something that can be funded. And ultimately, it becomes something that can impact not only your life, but the lives connected to what you are building.

Now it is time to begin.

Chapter 2: The Power of Writing It Down

"You do not write because everything is clear. You write to make things clear."

There is a difference between having a vision and communicating a vision. One exists in your mind. The other exists in a form that can be understood, evaluated, and acted upon by someone else. Most people never make that transition.

Research on goal achievement, including a widely cited study conducted by Dr. Gail Matthews at Dominican University, consistently shows that people who write down their goals are significantly more likely to achieve them — with results as high as forty-two percent higher than those who do not. Not because those individuals are more talented, but because writing forces clarity. When something is written, it becomes specific. It becomes measurable. It becomes real.

Without writing, a vision can remain flexible in a way that feels comfortable but is ultimately limiting. Once you write it down, you are forced to answer questions you may have been avoiding. You must decide what you are building, who it is for, how it works, and why it matters. Writing requires decisions, and decisions create direction.

What Writing Actually Does for Your Business

A vision in your head may inspire you. But a vision on paper does something entirely different. It creates the foundation for strategy. When your vision is written, it can be developed into a business plan. It can be shaped into narratives that speak to funders. It can be translated into standard operating procedures that guide how your business functions. It can be reviewed by others who can offer insight, support, and resources.

Once your vision is written effectively, it can reach places you cannot. It can be shared, reviewed, and considered in rooms you may never enter. It can be read by decision-makers who will determine whether your idea moves forward or remains where it started. Writing gives your vision reach.

Writing Reveals What You Do Not Yet Know

As you write, you begin to see what is missing and recognize what needs to be strengthened. That understanding builds confidence, not the kind that is based on emotion, but confidence rooted in clarity. It is the kind of confidence that holds up when questions become more detailed and expectations become higher.

Too many people delay writing because they believe they need to have everything figured out first. But clarity does not come before writing. Clarity comes through writing. You do not write because everything is clear. You write to make things clear.

Once you embrace writing as part of your process, you allow yourself to begin where you are. Your vision becomes a strategy. Your strategy becomes a plan. Your plan becomes something that can be presented, reviewed, and funded.

Do not see writing as something separate from your business. Writing is part of building. It is part of positioning. It is part of preparing your vision to function beyond you. Because at some point, your business will need to speak for itself. And when it does, what you have written will determine how it is understood.

Chapter 3: The Visibility Problem

"People invest in what they understand, and they support what they can see clearly."

There is a misconception that quietly discourages many entrepreneurs before they ever get started: if I were more talented, more experienced, or more connected, I would have access to more opportunities. I would have funding. I would be further along.

But in many cases, that belief is not accurate. The issue is not always a lack of talent. It is not always a lack of ideas. It is often a lack of visibility. And visibility is not about being seen everywhere. It is about being understood clearly in the right places.

Funding decisions are rarely made based on potential alone. They are made based on what can be understood, measured, and trusted. Decision-makers are not simply looking for good ideas. They are looking for clear, structured opportunities that align with their goals and demonstrate a path forward.

The Difference Between Being Overlooked and Being Unclear

If your vision is unclear, if your explanation is inconsistent, or if your documentation is incomplete, the person reviewing your work does not have enough information to move forward with confidence. It is not that they do not believe in what you are doing. It is that they do not have enough clarity to support it.

When you misinterpret a visibility issue as a lack of ability, you begin to question yourself unnecessarily. You begin to shrink your vision. You may even stop moving altogether, believing that you are not qualified for the opportunities you desire.

But the truth is often much simpler. You have not been clearly seen yet. And in many cases, you have not been clearly seen because you have not yet made your vision clear enough to be seen. That is a much more empowering position. Because clarity is something you can develop.

Clarity Is Your Advantage

Even within real barriers of access and representation, clarity remains a powerful advantage. When your vision is clearly written, when your plan is structured, and when your documentation is complete, you increase your ability to be considered in spaces where decisions are being made.

Clarity reduces friction. It allows the person reviewing your work to understand what you are building, who it serves, and how it will function without unnecessary effort. It builds trust. Trust is a critical factor in funding decisions. People invest in what they understand, and they support what they can see clearly.

This is why visibility is not about volume. It is about being positioned in a way that your message is clear when it reaches the right audience. You do not need to be everywhere. You need to be understood where it matters.

If someone encountered your work for the first time, without any additional explanation from you, would they understand what you are building? Would they know who it is for? Would they be able to see how it functions and why it matters?

If the answer is uncertain, that is not a failure. It is an opportunity — to refine your message, strengthen your documentation, and move from being unseen to being clearly understood.

Chapter 4: From Idea to Language

"Without clear language, your idea remains personal. With clear language, it becomes transferable."

Many people believe they understand what they are building until they are asked to put it into words. But when it is time to explain it to someone else, the clarity they felt internally does not always translate externally.

Language is what carries your vision from your mind into the world. Without clear language, your idea remains personal. With clear language, it becomes transferable. A transferable idea is one that can be understood by someone who has never met you, heard your story, or experienced your passion.

The Three Foundational Questions

What do you do? Who do you serve? Why does it matter?

When someone asks what you do, your answer should not require interpretation. It should be clear, direct, and easy to understand. When someone asks who you serve, you should be able to identify your audience with intention. Not everyone is your audience. When someone asks why it matters, you are being asked to define the value of what you are building.

What This Looks Like Across Different Businesses

Service-based consultant:

What do you do?

I help small business owners create financial systems that reduce stress and improve profitability.

Who do you serve?

Business owners who have been operating for one to three years and feel overwhelmed by their finances.

Why does it matter?

When finances are unclear, owners make reactive decisions that stall growth. My work brings order to that chaos.

Food entrepreneur:

What do you do?

I create allergen-free baked goods for families who have been excluded from traditional bakeries.

Who do you serve?

Parents of children with food allergies who want celebration-worthy options without the health risk.

Why does it matter?

Every child deserves a birthday cake. Our products make that possible safely.

Nonprofit leader:

What do you do?

We provide after-school mentorship and workforce readiness training for young men ages fourteen to eighteen.

Who do you serve?

At-risk youth in under-resourced communities with limited access to career guidance.

Why does it matter?

Without intervention, too many of these young men age out of the system without the skills or confidence to succeed. We change that trajectory.

Notice that in every example, the answers are specific. They name an audience. They define a problem. They state an outcome. That specificity is what makes language functional.

Refining Your Language Over Time

Clear language does not happen by accident. Very few people get it right the first time. You write it one way, then you realize it can be clearer. You adjust it, simplify it, and test it again.

Language also has a way of exposing what needs to be strengthened. As you attempt to explain your idea clearly, you may discover areas that are not fully defined. This is not a setback. This is insight. It forces alignment between what you think you are building and what you can actually explain.

Take the time to refine your explanation. Write it down. Read it back. Adjust it until it feels clear, direct, and complete. Then test it in conversation. Because at the end of the day, people cannot support what they do not understand. And once they understand it clearly, everything begins to move differently.

PART II — THE STRATEGY

Make It Plain. Build the Plan.

Chapter 5: Make It Plain

"Making it plain is not about removing substance. It is about removing friction."

In real situations, people are not studying your idea the way you have. They are reviewing it quickly, often alongside several other opportunities. They are scanning, not studying. That means your message must be understood without effort. This is what it means to make it plain.

To make something plain is to remove anything that slows down understanding. It is to communicate in a way that is direct, structured, and immediately clear to the person receiving it. Many people mistake complexity for depth. In reality, unnecessary complexity often creates distance. Making it plain is not about removing substance. It is about removing friction.

The Reader Test

If someone who knows nothing about your business can read your explanation and understand what you do, who you serve, and how it works within sixty seconds, your message is clear. If they cannot, it is not yet plain. Your goal is not to impress the reader. Your goal is to guide them.

Before and After: What Plain Looks Like

Before (unclear):

"We leverage a comprehensive suite of wellness-forward, community-centered frameworks to activate sustained behavioral modification through evidence-aligned programming."

After (plain):

"We help adults in underserved communities build healthier habits through free weekly nutrition and fitness programs held in neighborhood centers."

Before (unclear):

"Our platform delivers dynamic, end-to-end solutions for micro-enterprise stakeholders navigating fragmented resource ecosystems."

After (plain):

"We connect first-time small business owners with the funding, training, and legal resources they need to launch and grow."

Simpler, more direct, more memorable. Every word earns its place.

Share your explanation with someone who is not familiar with your work. Ask them to explain it back to you. Listen carefully to what they understand and what they miss. Their response will reveal more than your assumption ever will.

This is how clarity becomes precision. This is how your message becomes effective. And this is how your vision moves from being understood eventually to being understood immediately.

Chapter 6: Build the Plan

"A business plan is not meant to overwhelm you. It is meant to organize you."

At some point, your vision must be organized in a way that other people can evaluate it. When it is time for someone to make a decision about your idea, they are not evaluating your passion. They are evaluating your structure.

A business plan or grant proposal is not meant to overwhelm you. It is meant to organize you. When done correctly, it allows someone who has never met you to understand what you are building, why it matters, and how it will work.

Organizational Overview — Who You Are

Before anyone can support what you are building, they need to understand who you are. This section introduces your business in a way that establishes identity, legitimacy, and trust. You are not trying to impress the reader with complexity. You are helping them quickly understand what your organization is, what it stands for, and who is behind the work.

This section is where you clearly state:

- What your organization does
- Who it serves
- Where it operates
- How long it has existed or what stage it is in

If applicable, this is also where you briefly highlight your legal structure, such as LLC or nonprofit, and any relevant certifications or designations.

Example:

"Our organization was created to support working families who struggle to access reliable childcare. Based in Milwaukee, we serve parents in underserved communities who face daily challenges balancing employment and family responsibilities. Our team includes experienced educators and community advocates who understand these challenges firsthand and are committed to delivering consistent, high-quality care."

The Why Behind Your Why — Your Narrative
Your narrative explains why this work exists in the first place. This is where your purpose becomes clear, not just to you, but to the person reading your plan. It provides

context and meaning behind your business and helps the reader understand what led to the creation of your work.

This section should feel real and grounded. It is not about telling a dramatic story. It is about clearly connecting your experience, your observation, or your calling to the problem you are solving.

A strong narrative answers the question: Why did you choose this work, and why does it matter to you?

Example:

"After watching multiple parents in my community lose jobs due to inconsistent childcare, I realized this was not just an inconvenience. It was a barrier to stability. Families were not struggling because they lacked motivation. They were struggling because they lacked reliable support. This business was created to provide consistent childcare solutions where they are needed most, allowing parents to maintain employment and build stability."

Statement of Need — The Problem You Solve
This section requires honesty and specificity. You are clearly defining the problem your business or program is designed to address. You are identifying who is affected, what is happening, and why it matters right now.

This is not the place for general statements. The clearer and more specific the problem, the stronger and more credible your solution becomes.

Whenever possible, include:

- Data or statistics
- Local or community-specific insight
- Observable patterns or trends

Example:

"In our target area, over forty percent of working parents report missing work due to unreliable childcare. This results in lost income, increased financial instability, and a higher risk of job loss. For many families, the lack of dependable childcare is not a temporary issue. It is an ongoing barrier that limits their ability to maintain consistent employment."

Program Design and Activities — How It Works

This is where your vision becomes operational. You are explaining how your business or program functions on a day-to-day basis. The reader should be able to clearly see how your services are delivered and what the experience looks like for those you serve.

This section should answer:

- What you offer
- How it is delivered
- When and where it takes place
- Who is responsible for carrying it out

Clarity here reduces uncertainty and builds confidence in your ability to execute.

Example:

"We operate a mobile childcare service that travels to designated community locations during peak working hours. Our team provides safe, structured care for children ages two to ten, including educational activities, supervised play, and meal support where needed. Services are scheduled based on community demand, allowing us to meet families where they are and provide consistent support during critical working hours."

Measurable Outcomes — What Success Looks Like
This section defines how you will measure the effectiveness of your work. It answers the question: How will you know this is working?

Strong outcomes are specific, realistic, and measurable. They allow funders, partners, and stakeholders to evaluate the impact of your work objectively.

Whenever possible, include:

- Numbers
- Percentages
- Timeframes

Example:

"Within the first year, we aim to serve at least one hundred families, reduce missed workdays among participating parents by at least thirty percent, and maintain a satisfaction rate above ninety percent based on participant feedback. We will track attendance, service usage, and employment stability to measure overall impact."

Budget and Financial Plan — How the Money Is Used
This section explains how funding will be applied in a clear and responsible way. It shows that you have thought through the financial side of your operations and understand what is required to deliver your services effectively.

You are not just listing expenses. You are demonstrating intentional use of resources.

This section should reflect:

- Key cost categories
- Operational priorities
- Alignment between spending and outcomes

Example:

"Funding will support staffing, transportation, childcare supplies, and program coordination. These resources ensure that services are delivered consistently, safely, and at a level that meets the needs of the families we serve. Each expense category is directly tied to maintaining reliable service delivery and supporting measurable outcomes."

Organizational Capacity — Why You Can Do This

This section builds confidence in your ability to execute what you have outlined. It answers the question: Why should someone trust you to carry this out successfully?

You are highlighting:

- Your experience
- Your team's qualifications

- Any relevant partnerships
- Systems or processes already in place

This is not about overstating your credentials. It is about clearly showing that you are prepared.

Example:

"Our leadership team includes professionals with backgrounds in early childhood education, program management, and community outreach. Combined, we bring both technical expertise and lived experience in the communities we serve. Our operational structure supports consistent service delivery, and our team is equipped to manage both program quality and day-to-day logistics effectively."

Sustainability Plan — How It Continues

This section explains how your business or program will continue beyond initial funding. It shows that you are not relying on a single source of support and that you have a plan for long-term stability.

Sustainability can include:

- Revenue streams
- Partnerships
- Repeat funding strategies

- Growth plans

This section reassures the reader that their investment will not result in a short-term effort, but in something that can continue and expand.

Example:

"We will sustain operations through a combination of service fees, strategic partnerships, and ongoing funding opportunities. As the program demonstrates impact, we will expand into additional communities while maintaining service quality. Our long-term approach is designed to reduce dependency on a single funding source and create a stable, scalable model."

Bringing It All Together

When these sections are aligned, your plan becomes more than a document. It becomes a complete and cohesive picture of what you are building.

Each section supports the next. Your narrative connects to your need. Your need supports your design. Your design leads to measurable outcomes. Your outcomes justify your budget. Your capacity supports your execution. Your sustainability ensures continuity.

When everything works together, the person reviewing your plan does not have to search for clarity. They can see it.

That clarity allows them to move from understanding your vision to believing in it. It removes uncertainty and replaces it with confidence.

This is what makes your vision fundable..

Chapter 7: Answering the Money Questions

"When your plan is clear, your answers become clear. When your structure is strong, your communication becomes strong."

At some point, your vision will be questioned, not in a negative way, but in a necessary way. Most funding conversations come down to a small set of core questions. How you answer them determines how your vision is received.

How Does Your Business Make Money?

Example response: "We generate revenue through monthly service packages and partnerships with local employers who subsidize childcare for their staff." That answer shows structure. It shows that you have thought beyond the idea and into how the business operates financially.

Who Is Your Business For?

Example response: "Our services are designed for working parents in underserved communities who need consistent and affordable childcare options."

Why Now?

Example response: "With rising childcare costs and increasing workforce demands, more families are struggling to maintain stable employment. Our model addresses that gap by providing flexible, community-based solutions."

Why You?

Example response: "I have worked directly with families facing these challenges and understand the gaps in existing services. This business was built from that experience and is designed to meet those needs in a practical way."

What Happens If This Does Not Work?

Example response: "We have identified two alternative revenue streams we can activate if our primary model needs adjustment. Additionally, we have kept our startup costs lean enough that we can sustain operations while we refine our approach based on early market feedback."

How Will You Scale?

Example response: "Our model is designed to be replicated. Once we establish proof of concept in this community, we plan to expand to two additional markets within eighteen months using the same operational framework."

Preparation is what creates confidence in these moments. When your plan is clear, your answers become clear. When your structure is strong, your communication becomes strong. And that confidence allows you to stand in conversations where decisions are being made, not as someone asking for an opportunity, but as someone prepared for it.

How Funders Actually Think

Everything covered in this chapter has prepared you to answer questions. But before you walk into that room, submit that proposal, or click send on that application, there is one more shift that needs to happen. You need to understand what is happening on the other side of the decision.

Funders are not simply looking for good ideas. They are managing risk. Every dollar they award or lend is a decision they have to justify — to a board, to a committee, to a set of stated priorities, or to their own fiduciary responsibility. That context changes everything about how you need to present your business.

Risk vs. Trust

At its core, every funding decision is a trust calculation. The funder is asking one fundamental question: do I trust that this person and this organization can do what they say they will do with the resources I provide?

Trust is built through evidence, not intention. A funder cannot feel your passion. They cannot assess your work ethic through a conversation. What they can evaluate is what you have documented, what you have organized, and how clearly you have communicated your plan. Every element of your application either builds trust or introduces doubt. There is very little neutral territory.

Why Clarity Reduces Perceived Risk

When your vision is unclear, when your plan is incomplete, or when your financials are disorganized, the funder's brain registers that as risk. Not because you are a risky investment necessarily, but because they cannot see clearly enough to evaluate you. Uncertainty feels like risk, even when the underlying opportunity is strong.

Clarity does the opposite. When your plan is structured and your language is precise, when your outcomes are measurable and your budget is organized, the funder can evaluate you confidently. They can see the path. And when they can see the path, the decision becomes easier.

This is why two applicants with equally strong ideas can receive completely different outcomes. The one who communicated clearly reduced the funder's perceived risk. The one who left gaps introduced uncertainty. Funders move toward clarity and away from confusion, every single time.

What Makes Funders Say No Quickly

Experienced funders develop pattern recognition. Within the first few minutes of reviewing an application, they are already forming an impression. Here is what triggers a fast no:

- Vague or inconsistent language about what the business or program actually does

- A mission that does not clearly connect to the funder's stated priorities

- Missing documentation — no EIN, no registered entity, no financial records

- Outcomes that cannot be measured, making it impossible to evaluate success

- A budget that does not align with the program description

- A narrative focused entirely on need rather than capacity and plan

- Evidence that the applicant does not understand the funder's mission

None of these are fatal flaws in the business itself. They are failures of presentation. And every single one is within your control.

Why Incomplete Businesses Get Ignored

Funders are not in the business of building your foundation for you. They fund organizations that are already positioned to receive and deploy resources responsibly. If your business is not legally registered, your finances are not separated, or you cannot clearly explain your revenue model or governance structure, you are asking the funder to take on a level of risk that most of them are not authorized or inclined to accept.

This is not a judgment about the value of your vision. It is a structural reality. Funders invest in readiness. The more ready you are, the more fundable you become. And readiness, as this entire book has shown you, is something you build deliberately.

> **Funders are not evaluating whether your dream is worthy. They are evaluating whether your organization is ready. Readiness is what you control.**

Chapter 8: The Clarity Advantage

"Confidence is not the starting point. Clarity is."

There is a belief that quietly holds many people back before they ever begin. People tell themselves that once they feel more confident, they will move forward. It sounds good, but it is not how growth works.

Confidence is not the starting point. Clarity is. In reality, confidence does not lead. It follows. It develops as a result of understanding what you are doing and why you are doing it.

When you are unclear, everything feels uncertain. You hesitate, second-guess yourself, and question whether you are qualified or ready. But when clarity begins to take shape, something shifts internally. You begin to understand your own vision in a deeper way. You know how to explain it. You know who it is for. As that understanding grows, your confidence grows with it.

I have experienced this in my own journey. There were seasons where I had the vision clearly in my heart, but I had not yet taken the time to fully structure it. In those moments, confidence felt inconsistent. It was not until I slowed down and committed to writing, organizing, and structuring what I was building that everything began to align. As I gained clarity, I gained language. As I gained language, I gained direction. And as I gained direction, confidence followed naturally.

When you are clear, you move differently. You are not trying to convince people to understand something you cannot fully explain. You are communicating from a place of understanding. You know what you are building, and that knowledge changes how you show up.

I have seen this transformation in others. I have worked with individuals who came in unsure, hesitant, and overwhelmed. Once they took the time to write their vision, refine their language, and structure their plan, their presence began to change. They stopped shrinking in conversations and began to stand firmly in what they were building. Nothing about their intelligence changed. What changed was their clarity. And clarity created confidence.

When you shift your focus from trying to feel confident to becoming clear, everything begins to move differently. You begin to make decisions with intention instead of uncertainty. You recognize opportunities that align with your vision and avoid those that do not.

Release the idea that you need to feel ready before you begin. Your responsibility is to become clear. To write your vision. To refine your language. To build your plan. As you do, you will speak with more certainty. You will move with intention instead of hesitation.

That understanding is your advantage. This is the clarity advantage. And once you have it, you will not need to search for confidence. You will already be walking in it.

PART III — THE FUNDING BLUEPRINT

Positioning for Capital

Chapter 9: The 8 Funding Streams

"The goal is not to chase funding. The goal is to choose funding that aligns with your structure."

Once your vision is clear and your plan is structured, the next question becomes unavoidable: how do you fund it? The truth is, there is not just one way to fund a vision. There are multiple pathways, each serving a different purpose. Funding is not one-size-fits-all; it is strategic.

---

1. Personal Funding

Personal funding is the most immediate and often the most accessible starting point. It includes your own savings, income, or other resources you are willing to invest.

When to use it:

In the early stages when external funding may not yet be available. Personal investment demonstrates commitment and belief in what you are building.

Common mistake:

Investing personal funds without separating them from your business finances. Keep your business banking distinct from the start.

Benefit:

You maintain full control and can move quickly without waiting for approvals.

---

2. Bootstrapping

Bootstrapping is the process of building your business using the revenue it generates. Instead of seeking outside funding immediately, you reinvest your earnings back into the business.

When to use it:

Most effective when your business can generate income early, even at a small scale.

Common mistake:

Scaling too fast before the business model is proven. Every dollar reinvested should be tracked against a clear growth goal.

Benefit:

You retain full ownership and learn your business deeply by managing its growth from within.

---

3. Crowdfunding

Crowdfunding allows you to raise money from a group of people, often through online platforms such as Kickstarter, Indiegogo, or GoFundMe.

When to use it:

When your idea resonates strongly with a specific community and you have a way to tell a compelling story publicly. Crowdfunding is not just about funding — it is validation.

Common mistake:

Launching a campaign without a clear marketing plan or audience already in place.

Benefit:

You raise funds without giving up equity or taking on debt, while simultaneously building your customer base.

---

4. Angel Investors

Angel investors are individuals who invest their own money into businesses they believe in, often in exchange for equity or a return.

When to use it:

When your business has real growth potential and you are prepared to present a structured plan. Angels often bring more than money — they bring experience, networks, and mentorship.

Common mistake:

Approaching angel investors without a clear business plan or financial projections. Vague plans signal risk.

Benefit:

Access to capital and expertise from someone personally invested in your success.

---

5. Grants

Grants are unique because they do not require repayment. They are awarded by government agencies, foundations, corporations, or nonprofits aligned with a specific mission or purpose.

When to use it:

When your business addresses a defined need or serves a specific population that aligns with a funder's stated priorities. Alignment matters more than need.

Common mistake:

Applying for grants before your business is properly structured or documented. Funders verify legitimacy. If your business is not registered or lacks an EIN, most grants will disqualify you immediately.

Benefit:

Non-repayable funding that, when aligned properly, can provide significant capital without diluting your ownership.

---

6. Business Loans

Loans provide access to capital that must be repaid over time, often with interest. Lenders — banks, credit unions, or the SBA — evaluate your ability to repay before approving.

When to use it:

When you have a defined plan for how the money will be used and how it will generate return.

Common mistake:

Taking on debt without a clear repayment strategy. Model your projections conservatively.

Benefit:

Access to larger capital amounts than many grant programs offer, without giving up equity in your business.

---

7. Partnerships

A strategic partnership involves working with another individual or organization that brings resources — financial, operational, or strategic — to support your business.

When to use it:

When there is genuine alignment in goals and values. Strong partnerships can accelerate growth and reduce the burden of building alone.

Common mistake:

Entering a partnership without a written agreement. Roles, responsibilities, revenue sharing, and exit terms should be defined in writing before the relationship begins.

Benefit:

Shared resources, shared reach, and shared credibility — all of which can open doors that would be harder to reach independently.

---

8. Venture Capital

Venture capital involves receiving funding from firms that invest in businesses with high growth potential, typically in exchange for equity.

When to use it:

This pathway is not for every business. It typically requires a strong track record, a clear and rapid growth strategy, and willingness to give up a portion of ownership.

Common mistake:

Pursuing venture capital before achieving product-market fit or building a proven revenue model. VC firms fund growth, not ideas.

Benefit:

Large capital infusions that can accelerate growth dramatically, along with strategic guidance from experienced investors.

Many businesses use a combination of these approaches at different stages. The goal is not to chase funding. The goal is to choose funding that aligns with your structure. When your vision is clear and your plan is strong, you are making informed decisions about which path to take and when to take it.

Chapter 10: Grants — Alignment Over Need

"Grants are not awarded solely on need. They are awarded based on alignment."

Many people approach grants, prioritizing need over alignment. This misunderstanding creates unrealistic expectations and leads to frustration before the process even begins. There is a common belief that if the need is great enough, funding should follow. That belief sounds reasonable, but it is not how grants work.

Grants are not awarded solely on need. They are awarded based on alignment. Organizations that provide grants are making strategic investments. Every grant is tied to a mission, a set of priorities, and specific outcomes the funder is trying to achieve. The decision is not based on who needs the funding the most. It is based on which applicant best aligns with what the funder is already committed to accomplishing.

Eligibility Is Not the Same as Alignment

Many people apply for grants simply because they qualify on paper. When the application is denied, the response is often confusion. The reality is much simpler: the opportunity was never designed for what they were building.

Before you ever begin writing, you must understand the funder. Study their mission, their funding history, and the types of programs they support. A stronger approach is to begin with alignment. Instead of asking how to make your idea fit a grant, ask where your work naturally fits within existing funding priorities.

Where to Find Grant Opportunities

- Grants.gov — The primary database for federal grant opportunities in the United States: www.grants.gov.

- SBA.gov — Resources on grants and funding programs specifically for small business owners: www.sba.gov.

- Candid.org — Data on foundations, their giving priorities, and grant opportunities: www.candid.org.

- Foundation Directory Online — A searchable database of private and corporate foundation grants. Many public libraries offer free access.

- Local community foundations — Search for your city or county combined with the words "community foundation."

- Corporate grant programs — Many major corporations operate small business and community grant programs that are often under-applied to.

- MBDA Business Center — Resources for minority-owned businesses: www.mbda.gov.

Grant Readiness Checklist

- Business is legally registered with the state

- EIN (Employer Identification Number) is on file

- SAM.gov registration is active if applying for federal grants

- DUNS or UEI number is established

- Business bank account is separate from personal finances

- Business plan is written and current

- Financial records are organized and accessible

- Business licenses and permits are current

- You can clearly articulate your mission, population served, and measurable outcomes

- Your work aligns with the funder's stated priorities — not just meets eligibility requirements

If you are a nonprofit organization, confirm the following additional items before submitting any grant application:

- Board has met at least quarterly and meeting minutes are current and accessible

- A conflict of interest policy is in place and each board member has signed an annual acknowledgment

- The board has formally authorized this grant application by vote, documented in meeting minutes or a board resolution

- IRS Form 990 filings are current (or Form 990-N for organizations under $50,000 in annual gross receipts)

- Board roster is current with member names, terms, and contact information on file

- Bylaws are current, accessible, and reflect how the organization is actually operating

The Role of a Grant Writer

A strong grant writer helps you organize your ideas, strengthen your language, and present your proposal in a clear, structured way. However, a grant writer cannot create alignment where it does not exist. You bring the vision. You bring the understanding of the work. A grant writer helps you communicate that clearly, but they cannot replace your clarity.

Grants are not about convincing someone to give you money. They are about demonstrating that your work belongs within a specific mission. When your vision, your structure, and your positioning align with that mission, your application stands on stronger ground.

When Funding Is Denied

This is the part of the process that most books skip. They prepare you to apply but not to lose. And the truth is, denial is part of the process. It is not the exception. It is one of the most common experiences in the funding journey, and how you respond to it will determine more about your long-term success than any single application outcome.

> **A denial is not a verdict on your vision. It is data about your positioning.**

Why Denial Happens

Most denials are not about the quality of your idea. They fall into a small number of predictable categories:

- Misalignment — Your work did not connect clearly enough to the funder's stated priorities. This is the most common reason, and it is almost always correctable.

- Readiness gaps — Your application revealed that something in your foundation was missing. A document was absent, a registration was incomplete, or your financial records were insufficient.

- Competition — Many strong applications compete for limited funds. Sometimes an equally qualified applicant simply had a stronger alignment with that particular funder's current priorities.

- Timing — Some funders prioritize organizations at a specific stage of development. You may have been too early, or in some cases, further along than what they typically support.

- Narrative clarity — The story of your business was not communicated clearly enough. The funder could not follow the connection between the problem, your solution, and the outcomes you intended to produce.

How to Interpret Feedback

When a funder provides feedback, treat it as one of the most valuable resources available to you. Not every funder will offer it, but when they do, read it carefully and resist the urge to be defensive.

If the feedback says your outcomes were not measurable, that is not a criticism. That is an instruction. It is telling you exactly what to strengthen before your next submission. If it says your mission did not align with their priorities, that is not a rejection of your work. It is telling you to research alignment more carefully before you apply.

When no feedback is provided, you can still learn. Review the funder's publicly funded projects from the same cycle. Compare those organizations to yours. Look for patterns in what they funded. That comparison will reveal more than any rejection letter.

How to Reposition and Reapply

A denial from one funder is not a verdict on your fundability. It is one data point. Your response to that data point is what matters.

First, address what you can control. If the denial revealed a gap in your foundation, missing documentation, weak financial records, or an incomplete narrative, fix it before you apply anywhere else. Submitting the same application to multiple funders without addressing the core issue will produce the same result repeatedly.

Second, evaluate alignment before you reapply to the same funder. Some funders accept reapplications in subsequent cycles. If you plan to reapply, study what changed in their funding priorities, refine your narrative to reflect that shift, and make it clear in your submission that you have grown since your last application.

Third, do not stop moving. A single denial should never pause your funding pursuit entirely. Continue applying to other opportunities that genuinely align with your work. Diversify your funding strategy across multiple streams. Maintain momentum.

The entrepreneurs who ultimately secure funding are rarely the ones who succeeded on their first application. They are the ones who treated each denial as a refinement opportunity and kept going.

Chapter 11: Building a Fundable Business Foundation

"Funding responds to more than passion or potential. It responds to structure, credibility, and readiness."

At some point, every business reaches a defining moment where the question changes. It is no longer about whether the vision is good or meaningful. The question becomes: is your business actually ready to receive money?

Funding responds to more than passion or potential. It responds to structure, credibility, and readiness. A fundable business is one that can be clearly identified, carefully evaluated, and trusted to manage resources responsibly.

11.1 — Choosing the Right Business Structure

- Sole Proprietorship — Simple to establish, but offers no separation between personal and business liability.

- LLC (Limited Liability Company) — Provides liability protection and flexibility. One of the most common structures for entrepreneurs.

- Corporation (S-Corp or C-Corp) — Best for businesses seeking investment or planning significant growth.

- Nonprofit Organization — Opens access to grants not available to for-profit businesses. Requires a board of directors and compliance standards.

Helpful Resource: IRS Business Structures Guide — www.irs.gov/businesses/small-businesses-self-employed/business-structures

11.2 — Registering Your Business Properly

Once your structure is chosen, your business must be formally registered by filing a formation document with your state.

- LLC — You will file Articles of Organization (called a Certificate of Organization in some states). This document officially creates your LLC and is filed with your state's Secretary of State or Department of Financial Institutions.

- Corporation or Nonprofit — You will file Articles of Incorporation. For nonprofits, a separate IRS application for 501(c)(3) tax-exempt status must follow before most foundations will award grant funding.

- Sole Proprietorship — No formation document is required. If you operate under a name other than your

own, you may need to file a DBA ("doing business as")
registration with your county.

Once your formation document is accepted, you will receive
a State Entity ID number (sometimes called a DFI
number). Save this number. Some funders and lenders will
ask for it when verifying your eligibility. After registration,
request a Certificate of Good Standing from your state;
many funders require it as part of the application process.

---

*Key steps: file your formation document, save your State
Entity ID, request your Certificate of Good Standing,
apply for your EIN after state registration is confirmed,
and secure your business name consistently across all
platforms.*

Helpful Resource: Apply for an EIN —
www.irs.gov/businesses/small-businesses-self-
employed/apply-for-an-employer-identification-number-
ein-online

11.3 — Business Identity Numbers That Matter

- EIN (Employer Identification Number) — Your
  foundational business identity. Required for nearly all
  funding applications.

- State Entity ID (DFI Number) — Assigned by your state when you file your formation documents. Some state, local, and corporate grant programs require this to verify eligibility.

- DUNS Number (Dun & Bradstreet) — Used to establish and track business credit. Many grant programs require this.

- UEI (Unique Entity Identifier) — Required for any federal grant applications processed through SAM.gov. This has replaced the DUNS number for federal purposes.

Resources: Dun & Bradstreet — www.dnb.com | SAM.gov — www.sam.gov

11.4 — Business Credit vs. Personal Credit

- Early stage: Personal credit supports the business

- Growth stage: Business credit begins to develop through vendor accounts and credit lines

- Established stage: Business credit leads, and personal credit becomes secondary

11.5 — Building Strong Business Credit

- Vendor accounts that report payment history to business credit bureaus

- Business credit cards used responsibly and paid on time

- Trade lines established with suppliers or service providers

- Consistent, on-time payments across all accounts

11.6 — Financial Separation and Business Banking

Your business and personal finances must be completely distinct. This includes a dedicated business checking account, separate debit or credit cards, and clear financial records. Blending finances weakens your credibility and raises concerns during funding reviews.

11.7 — Licenses, Permits, and Compliance

Every business must meet local, state, and industry requirements. Non-compliance quietly disqualifies many businesses from funding opportunities because funders verify compliance before approving awards.

Helpful Resource: SBA License and Permit Guide — www.sba.gov/business-guide/launch-your-business/apply-licenses-permits

11.7a — Nonprofit Board Governance and Meeting Minutes

For nonprofit organizations, governance is not simply a best practice. It is a legal obligation and a funding requirement. When you incorporate as a nonprofit, you agree to operate under the oversight of a board of directors. That board is legally responsible for your organization. Board meeting minutes are the official record that your board is functioning, that decisions are being made properly, and that leadership is accountable to someone beyond itself.

States can revoke nonprofit status for failure to maintain proper governance. The IRS can flag an organization during audits if governance records are incomplete or missing. This is not a distant risk. It is a practical reality that affects nonprofit funding eligibility every year.

Why Funders Ask for Board Minutes

Board meeting minutes come up in funding conversations more often than most nonprofit leaders expect. Here is how it surfaces across different funding types:

Foundation grants frequently require board meeting minutes as part of the application or due diligence process. Funders want to see that the board reviewed and approved the budget, authorized the grant application, and is actively engaged in organizational oversight. Some foundations will not release funds until they receive a formal board resolution, a signed document authorizing the organization to accept the grant. That resolution only carries legal weight if the board is actually meeting and recording minutes.

Government grants through federal and state agencies assume you have a functioning board. SAM.gov registration, federal compliance requirements, and agencies such as HUD and DHHS have been known to audit nonprofits and pull funding when governance records cannot be produced.

Lenders and CDFIs — Community Development Financial Institutions that provide loans to nonprofits will ask for organizational documents, including bylaws, articles of incorporation, and evidence of board activity, before approving financing.

What Funders Specifically Look For
When a funder reviews your governance records, they are evaluating several things:

- Meeting frequency — Most nonprofit bylaws require at least quarterly board meetings. If minutes show only one meeting per year, it raises an immediate red flag about whether the board is truly active.

- Quorum — Minutes must confirm that enough board members were present to legally conduct business. This threshold is defined in your bylaws. Meetings held without quorum are not legally valid.

- Financial oversight — Funders want to see that the board reviews financial statements regularly, not just the executive director. Approval of the annual budget should appear in your minutes.

- Conflict of interest disclosures — Required annually under IRS Form 990 guidance. Sophisticated funders check for documented conflict of interest policies and annual board acknowledgment.

- Grant authorization — A board resolution specifically authorizing a grant application is sometimes required before or after submission. Without active board minutes, you cannot produce this document credibly.

What This Means for Your Organization

Many early-stage nonprofit founders incorporate to access grant funding but are not yet operating with the governance discipline that incorporation requires. They file the paperwork, obtain the EIN, open the bank account, and then never hold a formal board meeting. When they apply for their first significant grant and are asked for minutes, they either submit nothing or submit something informal that signals to the reviewer that they are not ready.

This is one of the most common and most preventable reasons early nonprofits are passed over for funding. The fix is not complicated. Hold your board meetings on a regular schedule. Take formal minutes at every meeting. Keep them organized and accessible. Maintain a conflict of interest policy and document annual acknowledgment by each board member. These are not bureaucratic formalities. They are the evidence that your organization is being run with the integrity and structure that funders expect before they invest in your mission.

> *Governance is not paperwork. It is the evidence that your organization is being led with integrity.*

Helpful Resource: BoardSource (www.boardsource.org) — a leading organization providing governance resources, sample meeting minute templates, and board management guidance for nonprofits.

11.8 — Staying in Good Standing

Ongoing responsibilities include annual filings, license and permit renewals, compliance deadlines, and accurate recordkeeping. Missed deadlines can lead to penalties or loss of status. Discipline equals eligibility.

11.9 — Documentation That Funders Expect

- A structured, current business plan

- Profit and loss statements, balance sheets, or bank statements

- A clear organizational chart or team overview

- Defined operational processes or standard operating procedures

- Program descriptions and impact narratives

When these elements come together, your business begins to take on a different level of strength and presence. A strong foundation removes many of the barriers that often go unnoticed. It replaces uncertainty with clarity and hesitation with confidence.

Funder Readiness Scorecard

Use this scorecard to assess where you stand right now. Be honest. The purpose is not to discourage you but to show you exactly where to focus your energy before you apply for funding.

Check Yes or No for each item based on where your business stands today — not where you plan to be.

Question	Yes	No
My business is legally registered with the state	☐	☐
I have an EIN (Employer Identification Number)	☐	☐
I have a dedicated business bank account separate from personal finances	☐	☐
My business name appears consistently on all documents and platforms	☐	☐
I have a current, written business plan	☐	☐
I can clearly explain what my business does in sixty seconds or less	☐	☐
I can clearly identify my target audience by name and need	☐	☐
I can state my revenue model — how my business makes money	☐	☐
I have measurable outcomes defined (what success looks like in 6 and 12 months)	☐	☐
My financial records are organized and accessible	☐	☐
My business licenses and permits are current	☐	☐
I have reviewed the funder's mission and confirmed alignment before applying	☐	☐
I can explain why my business matters to someone who has never heard of it	☐	☐
I have a sustainability plan explaining how my business continues beyond initial funding	☐	☐
I am prepared to answer: What happens if this does not work as planned?	☐	☐

Question	Yes	No
Nonprofits only: Board meeting minutes are current for the past 12 months	☐	☐
Nonprofits only: The board has formally authorized this funding application	☐	☐

How to Score Yourself

Count your Yes answers and find your funding readiness tier:

- 14–17 Yes answers — FUNDABLE. Your foundation is strong. Focus on alignment and narrative quality.

- 9–13 Yes answers — ALMOST THERE. Identify the gaps and address them before submitting applications.

- 8 or fewer Yes answers — FOUNDATION FIRST. Complete your foundation before pursuing funding. Use Chapter 11 as your action plan.

This scorecard is not a judgment. It is a map. Every No is a specific, actionable item. Work through the list systematically and your fundability will grow with each one you can check off.

Chapter 12: Positioning Your Business to Be Seen and Heard

"It is not enough for your business to be built correctly. It must also be presented in a way that allows others to find, understand, and engage with it."

A well-structured business that no one can see or understand will struggle to move forward. You can have the right foundation, the right systems, and even the right intentions, but if your business is not positioned clearly, opportunities will pass you by without explanation.

Positioning is what connects your work to the people who are looking for it. It is how your business shows up when you are not in the room. It is how decision-makers form an impression before you ever speak. The next step is not just building correctly, but making sure what you have built can be seen, recognized, and understood in the spaces where opportunities exist.

Positioning is not about being everywhere. It is about being clear in the right places.

Your Online Presence

Your online presence is often your first introduction. Before someone schedules a meeting, reviews your proposal, or considers your business for funding, they will look you up. That moment happens quietly, without notice, but it carries weight.

They are asking questions immediately.

Is this business legitimate?

Is it clear what they do?

Do they look prepared?

Your website should answer those questions within seconds. It should clearly communicate who you are, what you do, and who you serve without requiring the visitor to search for clarity.

A simple, direct statement such as, "We provide mobile childcare services for working families in underserved communities," immediately communicates direction. It removes confusion and creates understanding. When that clarity is supported by well-organized navigation, clear service descriptions, and accessible contact information, it builds confidence.

Your website does not need to be complex to be effective. It needs to be clear, current, and aligned with your message.

Your social media presence extends that first impression. It shows that your business is active, consistent, and engaged. It gives people a sense of how you think, how you communicate, and how you show up over time.

Consistency matters. If your website communicates one message and your social media communicates another, it creates doubt. If your messaging shifts from post to post without direction, it creates uncertainty. Clarity across platforms builds trust, and trust is what moves opportunities forward.

Your online presence should reflect the same message, the same audience, and the same purpose at every touchpoint.

Visibility Is More Than Being Seen

Many people believe visibility is about posting more, showing up more, or being on every platform. But visibility without clarity does not create opportunity. It creates noise.

True visibility is being understood quickly by the right people.

You are not trying to attract everyone. You are positioning your business so that when the right person finds you, they immediately recognize that your work aligns with what they need.

That is what opens doors. That is what leads to conversations. That is what moves your business from being present to being considered.

Your Elevator Pitch and Beyond

One of the most practical tools you can develop is your elevator pitch. It is a brief, clear explanation of what you do, who you serve, and why it matters.

It should be concise enough to deliver in sixty to ninety seconds, but strong enough to leave a clear and lasting impression.

A strong elevator pitch does not try to say everything. It focuses on what matters most.

Example:

"I help working parents in underserved communities maintain stable employment by providing reliable, mobile childcare services. We go where families need us most, directly to neighborhoods during peak working hours, so that childcare is never the reason a parent loses a job."

That statement is clear. It defines the audience, the service, and the impact. There is no guessing required.

Your elevator pitch should allow someone to immediately understand what you do and why it matters. If they have to ask multiple follow-up questions just to grasp the basics, your message is not yet clear.

This is not about memorization. It is about understanding your business well enough that you can communicate it naturally and consistently.

The Creative Pitch

There are moments when you have more time. Networking events, presentations, funding conversations, and partnerships all give you space to go deeper. This is where your creative pitch becomes valuable.

A creative pitch expands on your elevator pitch by drawing the listener into the problem before presenting the solution. It creates connection before explanation.

Example opening:

"Imagine being a single parent who finally landed a job after months of searching. Your first week of work arrives, and your childcare falls through. You have no backup plan. You call in. And when you do, that job is gone."

Then the transition:

"That story is not hypothetical. We hear it weekly. Our business exists because that should never be the reason someone loses their income."

This approach does something powerful. It allows the listener to feel the problem before they evaluate the solution. It creates understanding on a human level, which strengthens engagement on a practical level.

A creative pitch is not about performance. It is about connection. It helps people see why your work matters before you explain how it works.

Chapter 13: Using AI as a Strategic Business Tool

"You do not need to understand how electricity works to turn on a light. You need to know where the switch is."

This chapter is for you even if you have never used AI before. Even if the word "algorithm" makes your eyes glaze over. AI is already part of your world. When your phone suggests the next word in a text message, that is AI. When you search for something online and the results feel like they read your mind, that is AI. When a streaming service recommends a show you end up loving, that is AI. It is already working around you every day.

What Is Artificial Intelligence?

Artificial intelligence, or AI, is technology that has been trained to recognize patterns, understand language, and generate responses that feel human. It is not a robot. It does not have feelings or opinions. But it has processed an enormous amount of text, data, and information — books, articles, websites, conversations, business documents — and it has learned from all of it.

Think of it this way: imagine you hired a research assistant who had read every business book, every marketing guide, every grant writing manual, and every how-to article ever written. And that assistant was available to you twenty-four hours a day, responded within seconds, and never got tired or frustrated. That is essentially what modern AI tools offer.

What Is Machine Learning?

Machine learning is the process by which AI gets better over time by learning from patterns. Think about how a child learns to recognize a dog. The first time someone shows them a dog and says "dog," they learn one example. Over time, they see hundreds of dogs and their brain builds a pattern. Machine learning works the same way, but with data instead of life experience.

Here is what this means for you: the more consistently you use an AI tool, over time it picks up on your preferences, your communication style, and the kinds of results that are most helpful to you. This is not magic. It is pattern recognition applied to your specific usage. The more intentionally you use AI, the more value you get from it.

How AI Learns Your Voice — And How to Help It

One of the most powerful things that happens when you use AI consistently is that it begins to reflect your voice back to you. Your voice is your tone, your rhythm, and your perspective — the values, the passion, and the purpose behind everything you communicate. When AI generates content, it starts from a neutral position. Your job is to teach it to sound like you specifically.

Step 1: Tell AI Who You Are Before You Ask It Anything

The single most effective thing you can do is start every session by giving AI context about who you are and how you communicate. Think of it as introducing yourself before asking a favor.

EXAMPLE OPENING PROMPT:

My name is Dr. Kara Lock-Harris. I am a business strategist and founder of KLH Business Solutions. I help entrepreneurs move from vision to structure to funding. My writing style is professional but warm — I write in plain language, I avoid jargon, and I speak directly to the reader. When you help me write anything, please match this style.

Step 2: Share Samples of Your Own Writing

EXAMPLE PROMPT:

Here is a paragraph I wrote that represents my voice well: [paste your writing]. Please study this example and use this tone, structure, and style whenever you write for me.

Step 3: Correct It When It Gets It Wrong

When AI produces something that does not sound right, correct it. The act of correcting is what trains the pattern for the rest of your conversation.

EXAMPLE CORRECTION:

This is close, but it sounds too corporate. I would never use the phrase "leverage synergies." Please rewrite this in simpler, warmer language, as if I am talking to a friend who happens to need business advice.

Step 4: Build and Save Your Voice Guide

Once you have worked with AI a few times and found language that truly sounds like you, save a short Voice Guide that you can paste at the beginning of any AI session to immediately set the tone. It might look something like this:

> *"My name is [your name]. I run [your business]. My audience is [describe them]. My tone is [warm/direct/professional]. I use plain language. I avoid corporate jargon. I write in short paragraphs. My writing is rooted in purpose and always connects back to real impact."*

Step 5: Use It Consistently

The entrepreneurs who get the most value from AI are the ones who make it part of their regular workflow. They draft with it. They review with it. They brainstorm with it. The more consistently you use AI, the better the results become.

A Beginner's Guide to Prompting AI

A "prompt" is simply what you type into an AI tool to get a response. The quality of what you get back depends largely on how clearly you ask.

Be Specific.

Instead of "Help me write about my business," try: "Help me write a two-paragraph description of my business that explains what I do, who I serve, and why it matters, written in a warm and professional tone for a grant application."

Give Context.

AI does not know anything about you unless you tell it. Always include relevant background before making your request.

Tell It the Format You Want.

If you want bullet points, ask for bullet points. If you want three options, ask for three options: "Give me three different versions of my mission statement — one formal, one conversational, and one bold and motivational."

Iterate, Don't Accept.

Rarely is the first response the best one. Ask AI to revise, tighten, expand, or rewrite. The back-and-forth is where the real value lives.

Ask It to Think Like a Specific Person.

"Review my business plan as if you are a grant reviewer. What questions would you have?" This technique helps you identify weaknesses before you are in front of a real decision-maker.

AI Tools for Every Stage of Your Business

You do not need all of these. Start with one or two that match your most immediate needs.

Tool	Best For	Stage	Access
ChatGPT	Writing, brainstorming, business plan content, emails	All stages	chat.openai.com — Free; Plus $20/mo
Claude	Long documents, grant narratives, business plan review, detailed analysis	All stages	claude.ai — Free; Pro plan available
Gemini	Research, Google Workspace integration (Docs, Gmail, Sheets)	All stages	gemini.google.com — Free; Advanced via Google One
Canva AI	Logos, marketing graphics, presentations — no design skills needed	Startup & growth	canva.com — Free; Pro $13/mo
Copy.ai	Sales copy, website content, outreach emails, taglines	Startup & growth	copy.ai — Free tier; paid ~$36/mo
Notion AI	Organizing notes, SOPs, project management, meeting summaries	All stages	notion.com — AI add-on $10/mo
Grammarly	Proofreading, grammar, tone adjustment for proposals and applications	All stages	grammarly.com — Free; Premium $12/mo
Otter.ai	Transcribing meetings, recording client calls, auto-generating notes	Growth stage	otter.ai — Free (limited); paid $17/mo
Beautiful.ai	Professional pitch decks and	All stages	beautiful.ai — From $12/mo

Tool	Best For	Stage	Access
	investor/funder presentations		

> *Start with the free version of any tool before paying for anything. Most free tiers give you enough to determine whether a tool fits your workflow before you invest.*

AI for Every Stage of Building Your Business

When You Are Just Starting: Clarifying Your Idea

USE AI TO:

I have an idea for a business but I am not sure how to explain it. Here is what I am thinking: [describe your idea]. Help me turn this into a clear, one-paragraph business concept that explains what it is, who it is for, and why it matters.

When You Are Setting Up: Building Your Foundation

AI can explain legal structures, walk you through registering your business, and help you understand what documents funders typically expect. It can also help you create standard operating procedures — the documented processes that explain how your business functions.

SETUP PROMPT:

Help me write a step-by-step standard operating procedure for how a new client gets onboarded into my business. Here is how the process currently works: [describe]. Format it clearly so a team member could follow it without asking me questions.

When You Are Writing Your Business Plan

BUSINESS PLAN PROMPTS:

Write a Statement of Need for my business. Here is the problem I am solving: [describe]. Here is who is affected: [describe]. Please write it in a way that is specific, data-aware, and compelling without being dramatic. Help me write the Organizational Capacity section. Here is my background: [describe]. Frame this in a way that builds credibility and trust with a funder.

Important reminder: do not submit AI-generated content without reviewing and personalizing it. Use AI to build the structure, then add your voice, your story, and your specific details on top.

When You Are Looking for Funding

FUNDING PROMPTS:

Here is a description of my business: [describe]. What types of grants would most likely align with this work? What search terms should I use to find them? Review this grant application narrative and tell me: Is the alignment with the funder's mission clear? Are the outcomes measurable? What is the weakest section?

When You Are Marketing Your Business

MARKETING PROMPTS:

Write five social media captions for my business that I can use this week. My business does [describe]. My audience is [describe]. The tone should be [warm/professional/motivating]. Each caption should end with a call to action. Create a four-week social media content calendar for my business. I want to post three times per week on [platforms]. Include a mix of educational content, client stories, calls to action, and motivational posts.

When You Are Managing and Growing

OPERATIONS PROMPTS:

Help me write a professional follow-up email to a potential partner I met at a networking event. Here are the key points I want to communicate: [list]. Keep the tone warm and professional. I have a difficult conversation I need to have with a client who is unhappy with a deliverable. Help me think through how to approach it and draft a message that addresses their concern and preserves the relationship.

How AI Gives You a Funding Advantage

Artificial intelligence is not just a productivity tool. When used strategically, it becomes a direct competitive advantage in the funding process. Most of the entrepreneurs and nonprofit leaders you are competing against for grants, loans, and investment are not using AI to strengthen their applications. That gap is your opportunity.

Here is how AI specifically moves the needle in funding situations.

Writing Faster, Stronger Proposals

Grant narratives and business loan packages require clear, structured writing that answers specific questions in a specific order. AI can help you draft those narratives faster, organize your responses more logically, and produce a first version you can refine rather than starting from a blank page.

The key is specificity. Do not ask AI to "write your grant proposal." Give it your actual information and ask it to help you structure a specific section. The more context you provide, the more useful the output becomes.

Example prompt: "I am writing the Statement of Need section for a grant from [funder name]. Their priority is [funder priority]. My organization addresses this by [your work]. Help me write a compelling, specific, two-paragraph Statement of Need."

Improving Clarity Before Submission

One of the most powerful uses of AI in the funding process is as a clarity editor. Once you have written a section of your proposal or business plan, ask AI to review it from the perspective of someone who knows nothing about your organization.

Example prompt: "Please read this section of my grant narrative and tell me: Is it clear what we do? Is the problem we are solving specific? Are the outcomes measurable? What would confuse a reader who has never heard of us?"

This simulates the reader test described in Chapter 5, but at scale and with specific, actionable feedback. It will surface vague language, missing logic, and assumptions you did not know you were making before the funder encounters them.

Practicing Funder Feedback

You can use AI to simulate the review process before you submit. Ask it to read your narrative and respond as a grant reviewer or loan officer.

Example prompt: "You are a program officer reviewing this grant application for a foundation focused on [mission]. Read this narrative and give me the three most likely reasons this application might be denied, and what you would want to see strengthened."

This kind of pre-submission stress test can reveal gaps that would otherwise cost you the award. It is the closest thing available to having an experienced grant reviewer on your team at no cost.

Identifying Alignment Faster

Finding grant opportunities that genuinely align with your work is time-consuming. AI can compress that research significantly.

Example prompt: "Here is a description of my organization and what we do: [paste your description]. Here is the mission statement of this foundation: [paste their mission]. On a scale of strong, moderate, or weak, how well does our work align with their stated priorities? What aspects of our work should I emphasize in the application, and what aspects should I downplay or not mention?"

That kind of alignment analysis, done manually, might take hours of careful reading. AI compresses it to minutes. And identifying a weak alignment before you invest forty hours writing a proposal saves you time, energy, and disappointment.

> **The entrepreneurs who use AI strategically in the funding process will out-research, out-write, and out-position those who do not. That advantage is available to you right now.**

What AI Cannot Do — And Why That Matters

AI cannot replace your relationships.

Funding, partnerships, and business opportunities are built on trust, and trust is built through human connection.

AI can be wrong.

Always verify factual claims, particularly anything involving numbers, dates, or legal standards, with a reliable source or professional.

AI does not know your specific situation.

The more context you give it, the more relevant its responses become. But it does not know the specifics of your community or the nuances of your personal story unless you tell it.

AI-generated content is a starting point, not a finished product.

Especially for grant applications, business plans, and client-facing materials, what AI produces needs to be reviewed, personalized, and approved by you before it goes out.

Getting Started Today

1. Go to claude.ai or chat.openai.com and create a free account. Both take less than five minutes to set up.

2. Write your Voice Guide — a short paragraph that describes who you are, your business, your audience, and your communication style. Save it somewhere accessible.

3. Start your first session by pasting your Voice Guide and then asking one simple question about your business.

4. Read the response. If it is not quite right, correct it. Tell AI what to change and ask it to try again.

5. Keep going. Use it for your business plan, your elevator pitch, your marketing content.

Bookmark this chapter. Come back to it as your business grows and your needs change.

Artificial intelligence is not a shortcut. It is not a replacement for the hard work of building something real. But it is one of the most powerful tools available to entrepreneurs today, and it is accessible to anyone with an internet connection and the willingness to learn how to use it.

Use it wisely. Use it consistently. And always make sure that at the end of every AI-assisted process, what you put out into the world sounds unmistakably like you. Because your voice — your story, your perspective, your purpose — is something no AI can replicate. That is your unfair advantage.

PART IV — THE EXECUTION

From Paper to Provision

Chapter 14: The Vision Worksheet

"A vision becomes powerful when it is written, defined, and organized."

Now it is time to move from thinking to doing. A vision becomes powerful when it is written, defined, and organized. Before you go any further, pause. Take out a notebook or open a blank document on your computer. Give yourself space to think without distraction.

Take your time. Write your answers fully. Revisit them. Refine them. This is where your business begins to take form.

Part 1: Defining Your Vision

1. What Are You Building?

Example: I provide structured business planning and grant strategy services for early-stage entrepreneurs who need clear direction, organized systems, and a defined path to funding.

2. Who Do You Serve?

Example: I serve aspiring and early-stage entrepreneurs, particularly women and minority business owners, who have a vision but lack the structure and guidance to position themselves for funding.

3. How Does Your Business Work?

Example: I deliver my services through structured one-on-one consultations, strategic planning sessions, and customized business plan development.

4. How Does Your Business Make Money?

Example: I generate revenue through business plan development packages, grant writing services, consulting sessions, and educational workshops.

5. Why Does Your Business Matter?

Example: This work matters because many entrepreneurs have strong ideas but lack the structure and guidance needed to bring them to life.

Part 2: Strengthening Your Position

6. What Problem Are You Solving (Specifically)?

Example: I solve the problem of entrepreneurs having unclear business structures and incomplete plans, which prevents them from qualifying for funding.

7. What Makes Your Solution Different?

Example: My approach combines structured business planning with personalized guidance, ensuring clients not only receive a completed plan but also understand how to use it.

8. What Results Do You Produce?

Example: My clients walk away with a completed business plan and the ability to confidently pursue funding opportunities within 60 to 90 days.

Part 3: Planning for Growth and Funding

9. What Does Success Look Like in 12 Months?

Example: In 12 months, I will have served at least 75 clients, generated consistent monthly revenue, and successfully positioned multiple clients to secure funding.

10. What Do You Need Right Now to Grow?

Example: I need funding to expand marketing efforts, invest in technology, and hire administrative support to increase capacity.

11. How Will Funding Be Used?

Example: Funding will be used to support marketing campaigns, hire support staff, improve systems, and expand service delivery.

12. What Happens If You Do Nothing?

Example: Entrepreneurs will continue operating without structure, missing funding opportunities and struggling to sustain their businesses.

Part 4: Building Sustainability and Structure

13. Who Can Help You Grow?

Example: I can partner with local organizations, business networks, and community groups to expand reach and connect with potential clients.

14. What Systems Do You Need in Place?

Example: I need client onboarding systems, scheduling processes, financial tracking tools, and documented workflows to ensure consistency.

15. Are You Personally Ready to Lead This?

Example: I am committed to consistently showing up, learning, refining my approach, and building this business with discipline and intention.

Once you have completed these questions, take a moment to read everything you have written from beginning to end. What you are looking at is no longer a collection of thoughts. It is your business taking shape. These answers can now be expanded into your business plan, refined into your pitch, and used to position your business for funding.

What once felt like an idea is now becoming structured, defined, and actionable. You are not just thinking about your business. You are building it.

Chapter 15: Your 30-Day Activation Plan

"What you do in the next thirty days will determine whether your vision continues to live on paper or begins to take form in real life."

Clarity without action will leave your vision in the same place it started. You have done the thinking. You have done the writing. Now it is time to move.

Day 1: Make the Decision

- Complete your Vision Worksheet from Chapter 14 if you have not already.

- Identify ONE specific action that moves your business forward today.

- Write down the three biggest things keeping you from moving forward. These are not roadblocks — they are your work list.

Before the day ends, complete that one action. Completion creates momentum.

Days 2–3: Establish Your Legal Identity

- Research your state's business registration requirements.

- Choose and confirm your business structure (Sole Proprietor, LLC, S-Corp, Nonprofit).

- Verify that your desired business name is available in your state.

Days 4–5: Register and Get Your Numbers

- File your formation document with your state. If you are forming an LLC, this is your Articles of Organization. If you are forming a corporation or nonprofit, this is your Articles of Incorporation. File through your state's Secretary of State or Department of Financial Institutions website. Fees typically range from $50 to $200.

- Save your State Entity ID number once your filing is confirmed.

- Request your Certificate of Good Standing from your state portal.

- Apply for your EIN at www.irs.gov (free, takes less than 15 minutes online) after your state registration is confirmed.

- Begin your DUNS/UEI registration at www.sam.gov if you plan to pursue federal grants.

Days 6–7: Open Your Business Bank Account

- Bring your EIN, business registration, and a form of ID to your bank or credit union.

- Open a dedicated business checking account.

- From this day forward, all business income and expenses flow through this account only.

Week 2: Build Your Business Plan

- Day 8: Write your Organizational Overview and Mission Statement.

- Day 9: Write your Statement of Need.

- Day 10: Write your Program Design.

- Day 11: Write your Measurable Outcomes.

- Day 12: Write your Budget Overview.

- Day 13: Write your Sustainability Plan.

- Day 14: Review the full draft. Read it as a stranger would. Identify gaps and refine.

Week 3: Build Your Visibility

- Day 15: Secure your domain name.

- Day 16: Create a simple, professional website.

- Day 17: Create or update your business social media profiles.

- Day 18: Write and practice your elevator pitch. Record yourself. Listen back. Refine.

- Day 19: Develop your creative pitch for longer conversations.

- Day 20: Share your business publicly on at least one platform.

- Day 21: Ask three people who know your work to review your website and give honest feedback.

Week 4: Position for Funding

- Day 22: Research three grant opportunities using Grants.gov, Candid.org, or your local community foundation.

- Day 23: Evaluate each opportunity for alignment — not just eligibility.

- Day 24: Confirm your Grant Readiness Checklist from Chapter 10. Identify any gaps.

- Day 25: Begin drafting your first grant narrative or business loan package.

- Day 26: Review your business credit profile and personal credit.

- Day 27: Identify one potential strategic partner or network you will join this month.

- Day 28: Reach out to that partner or attend a local business networking event.

Days 29–30: Review and Recommit

- Day 29: Review everything you built this month. What is complete? What needs more work?

- Day 30: Write your 60-day goals. What will you accomplish in the next thirty days?

At the end of thirty days, your business should look different. Not perfect, but positioned. You should have structure where there was once uncertainty. You should have clarity where there was once confusion. More importantly, you will have built the habit of execution. That habit is what carries your business forward.

Chapter 16: The Discipline of Execution

"Execution is what separates those who move forward from those who remain in the same place."

There is a gap that exists in almost every business journey, and it is not caused by a lack of ideas, resources, or even opportunity. It is the gap between the start and the finish. Most people do not struggle with beginning. They struggle with continuing.

The beginning is exciting. There is energy, vision, and momentum. But as time passes, the work becomes less exciting and more demanding. The structure you created now requires consistency. The vision you spoke about now requires follow-through. That is where things begin to change.

Execution is where many people quietly disconnect from what they said they would do. Not all at once, but gradually. It does not feel like quitting. It feels like slowing down. But what is really happening is a shift away from discipline.

Fear as a Hidden Force

Fear often sits underneath this pattern, not always in obvious ways, but in subtle ones. Fear can show up as overthinking, where you spend more time analyzing than acting. It can manifest as perfectionism, where nothing feels ready to release. Fear does not always stop you from starting. It often stops you from finishing.

Execution requires you to move even when everything is not fully clear. Waiting for certainty will keep you in the same place. At some point, you have to be honest with yourself about what is actually happening. Not what you intended to do, but what you are consistently doing.

Discipline Is the Bridge

Discipline is what closes the gap. Discipline is not about intensity. It is about consistency. It is the decision to show up for your business even when it is not convenient, even when you are not motivated, and even when progress feels slow.

Execution creates evidence. Evidence builds confidence. Confidence reinforces discipline. That cycle is what moves your business forward.

Take a moment and reflect honestly on your own patterns. Where have you been inconsistent? What have you started but not finished? What have you delayed that you already know how to do?

Write your answers down. Because the answers reveal where your discipline needs to grow. Once you identify those areas, your next step is simple: choose one thing you will complete. Not start. Complete.

Completion builds momentum in a way that starting never will. Execution is what separates those who move forward from those who remain in the same place. The bridge between where you are and where you want to be is not more ideas. It is discipline.

Chapter 17: From Vision to Legacy

"Legacy is not something that happens at the end. It is something built through the decisions you make from the beginning."

By now, you have done more than gather information. You have taken time to think, to write, to organize, and to begin shaping what once existed only as an idea. The question is no longer whether you can build something. The question is whether you will.

You are no longer simply thinking about starting a business. You are standing at the beginning of building something that has the potential to outlive your initial effort. That is where the concept of legacy begins.

Legacy Is Built Through Daily Decisions

Legacy is not something that happens at the end. It is something that is built through the decisions you make from the beginning. It is not defined by how quickly you start, but by how intentionally you build.

When you begin to think in terms of legacy, your perspective shifts. You begin to consider sustainability, not just opportunity. You begin to think about impact, not just income. You begin to recognize that what you are building has the ability to influence others in ways that extend beyond your immediate reach.

Impact Is Measured in Service, Not Scale

Impact is not measured only by scale. It is measured by effectiveness. You do not have to reach everyone to make a difference. You have to serve well, consistently, and with clarity.

Many businesses begin with strong energy but do not last because they are not built with structure. Longevity requires discipline, systems, and the willingness to continue even when progress feels slow. A business that lasts is one that is maintained. It is reviewed, adjusted, and strengthened over time.

Stewardship

Stewardship is the way you manage what has been entrusted to you. Your vision, your resources, your opportunities, and your influence all require intentional management. Stewardship means using what you have wisely, not only for your benefit, but for the benefit of those connected to your work.

The tools have been given. The structure has been outlined. The path has been made clear. What remains is your willingness to continue.

Someone Is Waiting for What You Are Building

There are people you may never meet who are already connected to what you are building. They are experiencing problems you have been called to solve. Your business is not just an idea. It is an answer. An answer to a problem that is real. An answer to a need that is present. An answer that requires your consistency, your discipline, and your willingness to move forward even when everything is not fully in place.

When you begin to see your work in that way, hesitation loses its power. What you are building is no longer optional. It carries purpose, responsibility, and impact.

This is where vision becomes legacy. Not in a distant future, but in the daily decision to build, to refine, and to continue.

The clarity.
The structure.
The tools.
The direction.

What remains is your decision to act. Because somewhere, someone is waiting for what you have been called to build. And the answer they need is already in your hands.

The KLH Framework — Revisited

You began this book at the start of the framework. You end it having moved through every stage.

✓ WRITE | You have defined your vision in words others can understand.

✓ STRUCTURE | You have built a plan that organizes your idea into something fundable.

✓ POSITION | You have established the foundation, visibility, and credibility funders look for.

✓ FUND | You understand the funding landscape and how to navigate it with intention.

✓ EXECUTE | You have a plan, a scorecard, and a thirty-day activation path.

What comes next belongs to you.

Continue the Journey

This book gave you the framework. What comes next is the work — and you do not have to do it alone.

Dr. Kara Lock-Harris and KLH Business Solutions work directly with entrepreneurs, nonprofit leaders, and early-stage business owners who are ready to move from vision to execution. Whether you need help building your first business plan, positioning for a specific funding opportunity, or navigating the grant application process, KLH Business Solutions provides hands-on strategic support at every stage.

Services Available Through KLH Business Solutions

- Business Plan Development — Structured, fundable business plans built around your vision and positioned for real funding opportunities.

- Grant Writing and Strategy — Alignment-first grant research and proposal development for businesses and nonprofits.

- Funding Readiness Consulting — One-on-one strategic consulting to close the gaps between where you are and where funders need you to be.

- Manuscript Editing and Ghostwriting — Professional editorial support for authors and thought leaders ready to put their ideas into print.

- Speaking and Training — Workshop facilitation, keynote presentations, and business intensives for organizations, communities, and cohorts.

The Unfair Advantage

Join Dr. Kara and a curated community of entrepreneurs at The Unfair Advantage — a business intensive designed to compress years of learning into a single high-impact experience. For dates, locations, and registration, visit the website below.

To learn more, work with Dr. Kara, or bring her to your organization:

www.klhbusinesssolutions.com

Glossary of Key Terms

The following terms are used throughout this book. Understanding them will help you navigate funding conversations with greater confidence.

Angel Investor

An individual who invests personal funds into early-stage businesses, typically in exchange for equity or a future return. Angels often bring mentorship and networks in addition to capital.

Articles of Incorporation

The legal document filed with your state to officially create a corporation or nonprofit organization. For nonprofits, a separate IRS application for 501(c)(3) tax-exempt status must follow before most foundations will award grant funding.

Articles of Organization

The legal document filed with your state to officially create a Limited Liability Company (LLC). Also called a Certificate of Organization in some states. This is the first document you file, and everything else — your EIN, your bank account, your funding applications — follows from it.

Bootstrapping

Building and growing a business using its own revenue rather than relying on external investment or loans. Requires discipline but allows the owner to maintain full control.

Business Credit

A credit profile established in the name of a business entity, separate from the owner's personal credit. Built through vendor accounts, business credit cards, and consistent on-time payments.

Business Plan

A written document that describes a business's mission, operations, target market, financial projections, and strategy. Required by most lenders and funders as part of the application process.

Certificate of Good Standing

A document issued by your state that confirms your business is legally registered, active, and current on all required filings. Many funders, lenders, and grant programs require this before reviewing an application.

Crowdfunding

A method of raising money from a large number of people, typically through online platforms, by sharing your business idea or cause publicly.

DUNS Number

A nine-digit identifier assigned by Dun & Bradstreet used to establish and track a business's credit profile. Required by many grant programs.

EIN (Employer Identification Number)

A unique number issued by the IRS that identifies your business for tax purposes. Required for opening a business bank account, hiring employees, and applying for most types of funding.

Elevator Pitch

A brief, clear explanation of what your business does, who it serves, and why it matters. Typically sixty to ninety seconds in length.

Equity

Ownership in a business. When investors provide funding in exchange for equity, they receive a percentage of ownership in return.

Grant

Non-repayable funding awarded by a government agency, foundation, or corporation to a business or organization that aligns with the funder's mission and priorities.

Grant Writer

A professional who organizes, writes, and submits grant proposals on behalf of a business or organization. A grant writer strengthens communication but cannot create alignment where it does not exist.

LLC (Limited Liability Company)

A flexible business structure that protects the owner's personal assets from business liabilities while offering tax advantages and operational flexibility.

Measurable Outcomes

Specific, quantifiable results that demonstrate whether a business or program is achieving its goals. Required in most grant applications and business plans.

Nonprofit Organization

A legally registered entity that operates for a charitable or community purpose rather than profit. Eligible for specific grants not available to for-profit businesses.

SBA (Small Business Administration)

A U.S. government agency that provides resources, guidance, and loan programs for small business owners. Visit www.sba.gov.

State Entity ID (DFI Number / Registration Number)

A unique number assigned to your business by your state when you file your formation documents. Some state, local, and corporate grant programs require this number to verify legal registration.

Statement of Need

A section in a business plan or grant proposal that clearly defines the problem your business or program is designed to solve, supported by data or specific examples.

Sustainability Plan

A component of a business plan that explains how a business or program will continue operating and growing beyond its initial funding or launch period.

UEI (Unique Entity Identifier)

A twelve-character identifier assigned by SAM.gov. Required for applying for any federal grants in the United

States. Has replaced the DUNS number for federal purposes.

Venture Capital

Funding provided by firms that invest in businesses with high growth potential, typically in exchange for equity. Best suited for scalable companies with significant expansion plans.

Vision Statement

A clear, concise description of what a business is building, who it serves, and the impact it intends to create. The foundation of all business communication and planning.

Resources Appendix

The following resources are referenced throughout this book, organized by category.

Business Formation Documents

- Articles of Organization (for LLCs) — Search your state name + "Articles of Organization filing" to find your state's form and fee.

- Articles of Incorporation (for corporations and nonprofits) — Search your state name + "Articles of Incorporation filing."

- Certificate of Good Standing — Request through your Secretary of State or Department of Financial Institutions.

- SBA Formation Document Guide — www.sba.gov/business-guide/launch-your-business/choose-business-structure

Business Registration and Legal Structure

- IRS Business Structures Guide — www.irs.gov/businesses/small-businesses-self-employed/business-structures

- Apply for an EIN (free, online) — www.irs.gov/businesses/small-businesses-self-employed/apply-for-an-employer-identification-number-ein-online

- State Secretary of State offices — Search your state name + "Secretary of State business registration"

Business Identification Numbers

- SAM.gov (UEI registration for federal grants) — www.sam.gov

- Dun & Bradstreet (DUNS number and business credit) — www.dnb.com

- State Entity ID / DFI Number — Available through your state's Secretary of State or DFI business lookup database

Licenses and Compliance

- SBA License and Permit Guide — www.sba.gov/business-guide/launch-your-business/apply-licenses-permits

Grant Funding Opportunities

- Grants.gov — www.grants.gov (federal grant database)

- Candid.org — www.candid.org (foundation and nonprofit funding research)

- Foundation Directory Online — foundationdirectory.candid.org (available through many public libraries)

- MBDA Business Center — www.mbda.gov

- Search your city or county + "community foundation grants" for local opportunities

Business Credit

- Dun & Bradstreet Credit Builder — www.dnb.com/products/credit-monitoring.html

- Nav.com — Free business credit monitoring and funding match tool

Small Business Support

- SBA.gov — www.sba.gov (loans, counseling, and training programs)

- SCORE (free mentorship) — www.score.org

- Small Business Development Centers (SBDCs) — americassbdc.org

- Women's Business Centers — www.sba.gov/local-assistance/resource-partners/womens-business-centers

KLH Business Solutions
- www.klhbusinesssolutions.com

Common Mistakes to Avoid

After years of working with entrepreneurs across all stages and industries, I have seen the same patterns appear again and again. These are predictable, preventable, and often the difference between a business that moves forward and one that stays stuck.

1. Applying for Funding Before the Foundation Is Ready

No EIN, no business bank account, no registered entity — and then wondering why applications are denied.

The fix: Complete Chapter 11 of this book before submitting a single application.

2. Confusing Eligibility with Alignment

Just because you qualify to apply for a grant does not mean it was designed for your work.

The fix: Research each funder's stated mission and past awards before applying. Ask: does my work naturally fit here?

3. Keeping Business and Personal Finances Mixed

When finances are blended, you cannot accurately measure profitability, and funders immediately question your credibility.

The fix: Open a dedicated business bank account now —
not when the business grows, but now.

4. Writing the Vision Once and Never Revisiting It

If your vision statement, business plan, and pitch have not
been updated in over a year, they may no longer reflect
what you are actually building.

The fix: Set a quarterly review date. Every three months,
revisit your core documents and ask: is this still accurate?

5. Waiting to Feel Ready Before Taking Action

Confidence does not come first. Clarity does. And clarity
only comes through action.

The fix: Begin before you feel ready. The work itself will
build the confidence you are waiting for.

6. Relying Too Heavily on One Funding Source

Depending on a single stream creates vulnerability.

The fix: Build a funding strategy that identifies two or three
streams appropriate for your stage. Pursue them in
parallel, not sequentially.

7. Skipping the Business Plan

The business plan is for you first. It forces the clarity that
this entire book is built around.

The fix: Write your business plan before you need it. Use Chapter 6 as your framework.

8. Letting Inconsistency Become the Pattern

Inconsistency rarely looks like failure. It looks like life — until months have passed and nothing has moved.

The fix: Create a weekly non-negotiable. One hour. One task. One decision that moves your business forward.

About the Author

Dr. Kara Lock-Harris is a business strategist, author, and founder of KLH Business Solutions. With more than twenty-five years of experience in finance, she has spent her career understanding how businesses operate, how financial systems function, and what it takes to position an idea for sustainability and growth.

Throughout her professional journey, Dr. Kara became known for her ability to take complex business concepts and make them accessible. Long before launching her own company, she was helping individuals and small business owners organize their thoughts, develop business plans, and create financial strategies that made their visions actionable. What began as helping others informally eventually evolved into a calling that could no longer be set aside.

After losing her corporate role due to automation, Dr. Kara applied everything she had spent decades teaching others. That transition led to the founding of KLH Business Solutions — a firm dedicated to helping entrepreneurs build structured, fundable businesses with clarity and intention.

Today, Dr. Kara works with startups, nonprofit leaders, and growing businesses to develop business plans, grant proposals, and operational strategies that position them for real opportunities. Her approach goes beyond writing documents. She teaches entrepreneurs how to think, structure, and communicate their vision in a way that can be understood, evaluated, and funded.

She is a sought-after speaker and educator whose sessions are known for being practical, direct, and transformative.

Dr. Kara's work is grounded in a simple but powerful belief: vision alone is not enough. When a vision is written clearly, structured properly, and positioned effectively, it becomes something that can move, grow, and be supported.

For more information, speaking inquiries, or to work with Dr. Kara Lock-Harris and KLH Business Solutions, visit www.klhbusinesssolutions.com.

A Note on Sources

This book is grounded in the professional experience, practice, and direct client work of Dr. Kara Lock-Harris over more than twenty-five years in finance, business development, and entrepreneurship education. The frameworks, checklists, guidance, and tools presented throughout are original to her methodology and have been developed, refined, and pressure-tested through real-world application.

The book is practitioner nonfiction, meaning that its authority rests on lived expertise rather than on an academic literature review. Readers will not find footnotes or in-text citations throughout, as the overwhelming majority of the content reflects the author's own thinking, observations, and professional knowledge rather than conclusions drawn from external research.

Statistical References

Chapter 2 references research on the relationship between written goals and achievement. This finding draws on a widely cited study by Dr. Gail Matthews, professor of psychology at Dominican University of California, whose research on goal-setting and accountability has been published and referenced broadly in business and behavioral literature. Readers interested in reviewing her work can search: Matthews, G. (2015). "Goal Research Summary." Dominican University of California.

Chapter 10 and Chapter 11 reference compliance standards, governance expectations, and funding requirements for nonprofits. This guidance reflects established standards from the IRS, the National Council of Nonprofits, BoardSource, and general practice in the foundation and government grant sector. Readers seeking deeper governance resources are encouraged to visit BoardSource at www.boardsource.org and the National Council of Nonprofits at www.councilofnonprofits.org.

All other factual examples used throughout the book — including references to childcare statistics, workforce data, and funding patterns — are used as illustrative examples drawn from general practitioner knowledge and publicly available research trends. They are not cited to specific studies because they function as representative illustrations rather than research claims.

A Final Word on Expertise

The most valuable source behind this book is experience. Dr. Kara Lock-Harris has sat across from entrepreneurs at every stage, helped them organize their ideas, write their plans, and position themselves for real funding opportunities. What she knows about what works and what does not has been earned through direct engagement with the process this book describes.

If you are looking for the credential behind this content, you will find it not in a footnote but in the results of the people who have worked with her, and in the clarity you now carry as a result of working through these pages.